TOILETRIVIA

U.S. HISTORY

The only trivia book that caters to your everyday bathroom needs

by Jeremy Klaff & Harry Klaff

This book might contain product names, trademarks, or registered trade-marks. All trademarks in this book are property of their respective owners. If used, they are for non-biased use, and we do not encourage or discourage use of said product or service. Any term suspected of being a trademark will be properly capitalized.

Cover art by Stephanie Strack

About the Authors

Harry Klaff covered the NHL for *The Hockey News* and *Hockey Pictorial*, and reported for both the Associated Press and United Press International. He has written three books, *All Time Greatest Super Bowl*, *All Time Greatest Stanley Cup*, and *Computer Literacy and Use*.

Today, he is a retired Social Studies teacher from Brooklyn. Because he never went on a date in his adolescence, Harry had plenty of time to research useless facts and figures on everything ranging from history to pop culture. Moonlighting as a hockey scoreboard operator and baseball beer vendor, Harry had ample time to collect data.

Yet somehow, he got married. In 1977, Jeremy was born. Rather than being raised on a steady diet of carrots and peas, baby Jeremy was forced to learn facts from textbooks. His first word was "Uzbekistan." Throughout his childhood, Jeremy had a hard time making friends. When other kids wanted to play baseball, he wanted to instruct them about Henry VIII's six wives. After a failed career as a standup comic and broadcaster, in 2000 Jeremy fittingly became a Social Studies teacher. Today he brings trivia to the next generation.

Collect All Toiletrivia Titles

US History

World History

Pop Culture

Sports

Baseball

Music

and more!

Get the full list of titles at
www.toiletrivia.com

Acknowledgements

We at Toiletrivia would like to thank all of the people who made this possible.

- •The ancient cities of Harappa and Mohenjo Daro for engineering advances in plumbing.

- •Sir John Harrington for inventing the modern flush toilet.

- •Seth Wheeler for his patent of perforated toilet paper.

- •Jeffrey Gunderson for inventing the plunger.

We would like to thank our families for suffering through nights of endless trivia.

We would also like to thank the friendly commuters at the Grand Central Station restroom facility for field testing these editions.

Introduction

Here at *Toiletrivia* we do extensive research on what you, the bathroom user, wish to see in your reading material. Sure, there are plenty of fine books out there to pass the time, but none of them cater to your competitive needs. That's why *Toiletrivia* is here to provide captivating trivia that allows you to interact with fellow bathroom users.

Each chapter allows you to keep score so you can evaluate your progress if you choose to go through the book multiple times. Or, you may wish to leave the book behind for others to play and keep score against you. Perhaps you just want to make it look like you are a genius, and leave a perfect scorecard for all to see. We hope you leave one in every bathroom of the house.

The rules of *Toiletrivia* are simple. Each chapter has 30 questions divided into three sections...One Roll, Two Rolls, or Three Rolls. The One Rolls are easiest and worth one point. Two Rolls are a bit harder and are worth two points. And of course, Three Rolls are the hardest, and are worth three points. You will tabulate your progress on the scorecard near the end of the book.

The questions we have selected are meant for dinner conversation, or impressing people you want to date. With few exceptions, our queries are geared for the uncomfortable situations that life throws at you, like when you have nothing in common with someone, and need to offer some clever banter. We hope that the facts you learn in the restroom make it easier to meet your future in-laws, or deal with that hairdresser who just won't stop talking to you.

Remember, *Toiletrivia* is a game. No joysticks, no computer keyboards...just you, your toilet, and a pen; the way nature intended it. So good luck. We hope you are triumphant.

DIRECTIONS

Each set of questions has an answer sheet opposite it. Write your answers in the first available column to the right. When you are done with a set of 10 questions, *fold* your answer column underneath so the next restroom user doesn't see your answers. *Special note to restroom users 2 and 3: No cheating! And the previous person's answers might be wrong!*

Then check your responses with the answer key in the back of the book. Mark your right answers with a check, and your wrong answers with an "x." Then go to the scorecard on pages 98-100 and tabulate your results. These totals will be the standard for other users to compare.

Be sure to look online for other Toiletrivia titles
Visit us at www.toiletrivia.com

Table of Contents

The Road to Independence

Flip to pg. 68 for answers

 ## One Roll

1. Who wrote, "These are the times that try men's souls"? One might say that he really used his *Common Sense.*

2. Who was the leader of the Sons of Liberty? Rumor has it that he enjoyed a good brew.

3. Who were the German troops hired by the King to fight against the Americans?

4. Where were the first shots of the Revolutionary War fired?

5. Who said "Give me liberty or give me death"?

6. How many lanterns did Paul Revere see in the steeple of Old North Church?

7. In what city was the Declaration of Independence signed?

8. Who was the King of England at the time of the American Revolution?

9. What American general conspired to turn West Point over to the British? What a turncoat!

10. What were the Boston Tea Partiers disguised as?

Answer Sheet | # Answer Sheet | # Answer Sheet

The Road to Independence | **The Road to Independence** | **The Road to Independence**
1 Roll | **1 Roll** | **1 Roll**

Name_____ | Name_____ | Name_____

1.	1.	1.
2.	2.	2.
3.	3.	3.
4.	4.	4.
5.	5.	5.
6.	6.	6.
7.	7.	7.
8.	8.	8.
9.	9.	9.
10.	10.	10.

After you have filled out the sheet, fold your column underneath along the dashed line so the next restroom user won't see your answers. ***The first player uses the far right column.***

Notes: | *Notes:* | *Notes:*

The Road to Independence

Two Rolls

Flip to pg. 69 for answers

1. Who was George Washington's aide-de-camp who later became a member of his cabinet?

2. What two Revolution leaders were Paul Revere (and others) sent to warn that the "British are coming"?

3. Name one other person besides Thomas Jefferson who was on the committee to write a formal Declaration of Independence.

4. Name the aristocratic Frenchman, who at age 19 joined the American cause.

5. What was the name of the battle fought in what is now part of New York City on August 27, 1776?

6. What was the name of the document which governed the United States from the end of the Revolutionary War until the Constitution was ratified in 1789?

7. Patriots were those who supported the colonists. What "T" word was used to describe colonists who stayed loyal to the British Crown?

8. For decades, two major cities celebrated Evacuation Day to commemorate the final removal of British troops. Name one.

9. Why did John Hancock allegedly sign the Declaration of Independence so large?

10. What did Benjamin Franklin want the national bird to be?

Answer Sheet

The Road to Independence
2 Rolls

Name_____

Answer Sheet

The Road to Independence
2 Rolls

Name_____

Answer Sheet

The Road to Independence
2 Rolls

Name_____

1.	1.	1.
2.	2.	2.
3.	3.	3.
4.	4.	4.
5.	5.	5.
6.	6.	6.
7.	7.	7.
8.	8.	8.
9.	9.	9.
10.	10.	10.

After you have filled out the sheet, fold your column underneath along the dashed line so the next restroom user won't see your answers. ***The first player uses the far right column.***

Notes: *Notes:*   *Notes:*

The Road to Independence

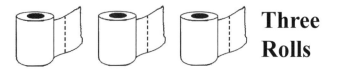

Three Rolls

Flip to pg. 70 for answers

1. Within 5, how many people signed the Declaration of Independence?

2. Within 30, how many cases of tea were dumped into Boston Harbor as part of the Boston Tea Party?

3. Identify who said, "I only regret that I have but one life to lose for my country."

4. Who was the leader of the British troops at the beginning of the Revolutionary War?

5. From what British fort did Ethan Allen confiscate cannons and bring them to Boston?

6. What future US President was involved in the Battle of Hanging Rock in South Carolina in 1780 at the age of 13?

7. Who was the first person killed at the Boston Massacre of 1770?

8. Who spent considerable time in the Netherlands during the Revolutionary War trying to get the Dutch government to give financial aid to the Americans?

9. What was name of the conspiracy that looked to remove George Washington from command, and replace him with Horatio Gates?

10. Polish-American Days are often named after this general who led American troops during the War. Who was he?

Answer Sheet

The Road to Independence
3 Rolls

Name_____

Answer Sheet

The Road to Independence
3 Rolls

Name_____

Answer Sheet

The Road to Independence
3 Rolls

Name_____

1.	1.	1.
2.	2.	2.
3.	3.	3.
4.	4.	4.
5.	5.	5.
6.	6.	6.
7.	7.	7.
8.	8.	8.
9.	9.	9.
10.	10.	10.

After you have filled out the sheet, fold your column underneath along the dashed line so the next restroom user won't see your answers. ***The first player uses the far right column.***

Notes: *Notes:*   *Notes:*

The Young Nation

 One Roll

Flip to pg. 71 for answers

1. How many people voted against George Washington to be the nation's first President?

2. Who was the first Secretary of War in US History? He was a rotund man, whose clothes could probably hold a lot of gold.

3. Which war saw parts of Washington, DC burned to the ground?

4. Who was the first President to sleep in the White House?

5. Who was nicknamed the "Father of the Constitution?"

6. Who was the first Chief Justice of the US Supreme Court? His first and last names started with the same letter.

7. Which Native American woman helped navigate part of Lewis and Clark's trip across the country?

8. What was the nickname of the USS *Constitution*, because cannon balls bounced off its sides?

9. Which future US President was the hero of the Battle of New Orleans?

10. What was the first state to be added to the Union after the original 13? American pancakes were no longer dry.

Answer Sheet

The Young Nation
1 Roll

Name_____

1.
2.
3.
4.
5.
6.
7.
8.
9.
10.

Answer Sheet

The Young Nation
1 Roll

Name_____

1.
2.
3.
4.
5.
6.
7.
8.
9.
10.

Answer Sheet

The Young Nation
1 Roll

Name_____

1.
2.
3.
4.
5.
6.
7.
8.
9.
10.

After you have filled out the sheet, fold your column underneath along the dashed line so the next restroom user won't see your answers. ***The first player uses the far right column.***

Notes:

Notes:

Notes:

The Young Nation

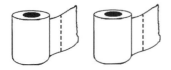

Two Rolls

Flip to pg. 72 for answers

1. Where was George Washington first inaugurated in 1789?

2. Which two Presidents and signers of the Declaration of Independence died on the same day—July 4, 1826—exactly 50 years to the day after its issuance?

3. Where was Francis Scott Key when he wrote the words to what would one day become *The Star Spangled Banner*?

4. Which 1786-87 rebellion in Massachusetts exposed weaknesses of the Articles of Confederation, and led to conventions to scrap them?

5. In order, what were the three capitals of the US?

6. What were the first two political parties in American History?

7. What fraction of a person did the founding fathers agree slaves would count for in a census?

8. Which was the first Presidential Election to be decided by the House of Representatives?

9. Which former Vice President was arrested in 1807 on charges of treason?

10. Which first lady, known to serve ice cream at the White House, saved Gilbert Stuart's famous portrait of George Washington during the War of 1812?

Answer Sheet

The Young Nation
2 Rolls

Name_____

Answer Sheet

The Young Nation
2 Rolls

Name_____

Answer Sheet

The Young Nation
2 Rolls

Name_____

1.	1.	1.
2.	2.	2.
3.	3.	3.
4.	4.	4.
5.	5.	5.
6.	6.	6.
7.	7.	7.
8.	8.	8.
9.	9.	9.
10.	10.	10.

After you have filled out the sheet, fold your column underneath along the dashed line so the next restroom user won't see your answers. *The first player uses the far right column.*

Notes: *Notes:*   *Notes:*

The Young Nation

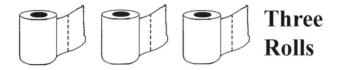

Three Rolls

Flip to pg. 73 for answers

1. Which two future presidents co-wrote the Virginia and Kentucky Resolutions?

2. How much money did the Louisiana Purchase cost?

3. Where was the duel between Alexander Hamilton and Aaron Burr held?

4. What state saw the Whiskey Rebellion of 1794?

5. Within 5, how many delegates were at the Constitutional Convention in 1787?

6. Which three Founding Fathers met for dinner to decide where the nation's capital would move?

7. Which French diplomat were Americans trying to negotiate with in the XYZ Affair?

8. Who wrote most of the Articles of Confederation?

9. Who can be considered to be the first President of the US because he was President of Congress in the early days of the Articles of Confederation?

10. Name the French national who in 1793 took it upon himself to try to recruit an army to invade Florida, Louisiana, and Canada.

Answer Sheet

The Young Nation
3 Rolls

Name_____

Answer Sheet

The Young Nation
3 Rolls

Name_____

Answer Sheet

The Young Nation
3 Rolls

Name_____

1.	1.	1.
2.	2.	2.
3.	3.	3.
4.	4.	4.
5.	5.	5.
6.	6.	6.
7.	7.	7.
8.	8.	8.
9.	9.	9.
10.	10.	10.

After you have filled out the sheet, fold your column underneath along the dashed line so the next restroom user won't see your answers. ***The first player uses the far right column.***

Notes: *Notes:*   *Notes:*

The Civil War

 One Roll

Flip to pg. 74 for answers

1. What was the bloodiest single day of the Civil War?

2. What was the turning point of the Civil War?

3. What were the two famous iron-clad ships of the Civil War that battled on March 9, 1862? They both began with the same letter.

4. During what years was the Civil War fought?

5. Who was President of the Confederacy?

6. Which was the first state to secede from the Union? Fittingly, the war also began in that state.

7. What was the colorful name of the federal paper currency during the war? The Confederates were *green* with envy.

8. What state had the first recognized African American regiment comprised mostly of Northern free blacks? Perhaps you saw the movie, *Glory*.

9. What was Thomas J. Jackson's nickname?

10. Where did Robert E. Lee surrender to Ulysses S. Grant?

Answer Sheet

The Civil War
1 Roll

Name_____

Answer Sheet

The Civil War
1 Roll

Name_____

Answer Sheet

The Civil War
1 Roll

Name_____

1.	1.	1.
2.	2.	2.
3.	3.	3.
4.	4.	4.
5.	5.	5.
6.	6.	6.
7.	7.	7.
8.	8.	8.
9.	9.	9.
10.	10.	10.

After you have filled out the sheet, fold your column underneath along the dashed line so the next restroom user won't see your answers. *The first player uses the far right column.*

Notes: *Notes:*   *Notes:*

The Civil War

Two Rolls

Flip to pg. 75 for answers

1. What alleged inventor of baseball was present at Fort Sumter?

2. By the end of the war, how many stars were on the Confederate Battle Flag?

3. What derogatory nickname did opponents place on Gen. Ulysses S. Grant because he threw unfit troops into battle, resulting in many casualties?

4. In what city did Abraham Lincoln sit in Jefferson Davis's chair?

5. What was the Confederate Army looking for when it marched into Gettysburg?

6. Which Army of the Potomac Commander did not act decisively when he was brought cigars wrapped in Lee's battle plans?

7. What did John Wilkes Booth yell when he leaped onto the stage after he shot Abraham Lincoln?

8. What song that's still a synonym for "The South," was written by a Northerner?

9. Which city had the bloodiest draft riot in response to the conscription of soldiers?

10. What snake was used to name the plan of the Union blockade?

Answer Sheet

The Civil War
2 Rolls

Name_____

Answer Sheet

The Civil War
2 Rolls

Name_____

Answer Sheet

The Civil War
2 Rolls

Name_____

1.	1.	1.
2.	2.	2.
3.	3.	3.
4.	4.	4.
5.	5.	5.
6.	6.	6.
7.	7.	7.
8.	8.	8.
9.	9.	9.
10.	10.	10.

After you have filled out the sheet, fold your column underneath along the dashed line so the next restroom user won't see your answers. *The first player uses the far right column.*

Notes: *Notes:*   *Notes:*

The Civil War

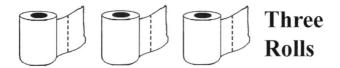

Three Rolls

Flip to pg. 76 for answers

1. Approximately how many slaves did the Emancipation Proclamation free?

2. Who was the first commander of the Union Army in 1861?

3. Whose "Raiders" was Jesse James a part of in the west during the Civil War?

4. Whose property did the Civil War begin and end on?

5. Why couldn't the Union retreat from Bull Run?

6. Where did the biggest man-made explosion in the history of the Western Hemisphere (to its day) take place?

7. What was the common name for the two ships being built in England that were ticketed for the Confederacy?

8. Which political general, and future Presidential candidate of the Greenback Party, is credited with the idea of confiscating Southern slaves for the Union cause?

9. What two cities make up the largest Civil War battlefield national park?

10. What battlefield is known for the Cornfield, the Bloody Lane, and Burnside's Bridge?

Answer Sheet
The Civil War
3 Rolls

Name_____

Answer Sheet
The Civil War
3 Rolls

Name_____

Answer Sheet
The Civil War
3 Rolls

Name_____

1.	1.	1.
2.	2.	2.
3.	3.	3.
4.	4.	4.
5.	5.	5.
6.	6.	6.
7.	7.	7.
8.	8.	8.
9.	9.	9.
10.	10.	10.

After you have filled out the sheet, fold your column underneath along the dashed line so the next restroom user won't see your answers. *The first player uses the far right column.*

Notes: *Notes:*   *Notes:*

The 20th Century

 ## One Roll

Flip to pg. 77 for answers

1. What was the name of the judge in the O.J. Simpson criminal murder trial?

2. What was the name of the German blimp which exploded over Lakehurst, NJ on May 6, 1937?

3. What event made Al Capone a national celebrity on February 14, 1929?

4. What court case ended segregation in schools in 1954?

5. What cruise liner was sunk by a German U-boat on May 7, 1915?

6. What city claims that aliens allegedly landed near it in 1947?

7. What holiday did Franklin Delano Roosevelt move in 1939 so retailers would have an extra week to sell their items?

8. What name was given to rebellious young ladies of the Roaring 20s?

9. On whose inauguration day were the Iran Hostages freed after more than a year of captivity?

10. Who delivered the *Ich Bin Eine Berliner* speech?

Answer Sheet

The 20th Century
1 Roll

Name_____

Answer Sheet

The 20th Century
1 Roll

Name_____

Answer Sheet

The 20th Century
1 Roll

Name_____

1.	1.	1.
2.	2.	2.
3.	3.	3.
4.	4.	4.
5.	5.	5.
6.	6.	6.
7.	7.	7.
8.	8.	8.
9.	9.	9.
10.	10.	10.

After you have filled out the sheet, fold your column underneath along the dashed line so the next restroom user won't see your answers. *The first player uses the far right column.*

Notes: *Notes:*   *Notes:*

The 20th Century

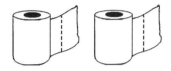

Two Rolls

Flip to pg. 78 for answers

1. What was the name of Charles Lindbergh's plane that took off from Roosevelt Field, Long Island?

2. What was the name of the plane that dropped the first atomic bomb on Hiroshima, Japan?

3. What was the name of Theodore Roosevelt's political party when he ran for President in 1912?

4. What famous Upton Sinclair book detailed the horrors of the meat packing industry?

5. Who assassinated John Lennon?

6. Upon its completion on May 20, 1930, what building in New York City became the tallest in the world? It's not the Empire State Building!

7. What was FDR's dog's name?

8. Which four Presidents are on the façade of Mount Rushmore?

9. What is the science fiction nickname for Ronald Reagan's "Strategic Defense Initiative?"

10. What "blew its top" on May 18, 1980 in Washington State?

Answer Sheet | Answer Sheet | Answer Sheet

The 20th Century
2 Rolls

The 20th Century
2 Rolls

The 20th Century
2 Rolls

Name_____ Name_____ Name_____

1.	1.	1.
2.	2.	2.
3.	3.	3.
4.	4.	4.
5.	5.	5.
6.	6.	6.
7.	7.	7.
8.	8.	8.
9.	9.	9.
10.	10.	10.

After you have filled out the sheet, fold your column underneath along the dashed line so the next restroom user won't see your answers. ***The first player uses the far right column.***

Notes: |*Notes:* |*Notes:*

The 20th Century

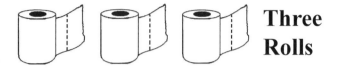

Three Rolls

Flip to pg. 79 for answers

1. Who were the two opposing attorneys in the Scopes Trial?

2. *The Grapes of Wrath* was written in response to what 20th Century natural phenomenon?

3. Who was the first President to step foot outside of the continental United States while in office?

4. What was the first dot.com domain ever registered?

5. Which toy company is given credit for inventing the Hula Hoop and Frisbee?

6. Name the town where the April 20, 1914 massacre of coal miners striking against the Rockefeller-family owned Colorado Fuel and Iron Company took place.

7. Who was the pilot of the U2 spyplane?

8. Who took the "Fall" for the Teapot Dome Scandal (first name please)?

9. After WWII, who devised the plan to give European nations economic aid to prevent them from turning communist?

10. Why did Theodore Roosevelt briefly suspend his campaign for President on Oct. 14, 1912?

Answer Sheet

The 20th Century
3 Rolls

Name_____

Answer Sheet

The 20th Century
3 Rolls

Name_____

Answer Sheet

The 20th Century
3 Rolls

Name_____

1.	1.	1.
2.	2.	2.
3.	3.	3.
4.	4.	4.
5.	5.	5.
6.	6.	6.
7.	7.	7.
8.	8.	8.
9.	9.	9.
10.	10.	10.

After you have filled out the sheet, fold your column underneath along the dashed line so the next restroom user won't see your answers. *The first player uses the far right column.*

Notes: *Notes:*   *Notes:*

Presidents

 One Roll

Flip to pg. 80 for answers

1. Which President served the shortest length of time?

2. Who was "*First* in War, *First* in Peace, and *First* in the Hearts of his Countrymen"?

3. Who was the first Catholic President?

4. Besides Bill Clinton, who was the only other President to be impeached?

5. Who was the first President to be assassinated?

6. Who was the only person to serve two non-consecutive terms?

7. Who was the first President to live to see his son become President?

8. Who was the first President after Washington to serve two full terms?

9. Which President was better known as "Ike?"

10. Who was the only President elected to a third (and fourth) term?

Answer Sheet

Presidents
1 Roll

Name_____

Answer Sheet

Presidents
1 Roll

Name_____

Answer Sheet

Presidents
1 Roll

Name_____

1.	1.	1.
2.	2.	2.
3.	3.	3.
4.	4.	4.
5.	5.	5.
6.	6.	6.
7.	7.	7.
8.	8.	8.
9.	9.	9.
10.	10.	10.

After you have filled out the sheet, fold your column underneath along the dashed line so the next restroom user won't see your answers. ***The first player uses the far right column.***

Notes: *Notes:*   *Notes:*

Presidents

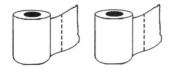

Two Rolls

Flip to pg. 81 for answers

1. Who was President during the Mexican War?

2. Who was the first President born in a log cabin?

3. What President was famous for his 1823 *Doctrine*?

4. Which President said, "I do not choose to run," in 1928?

5. What was "S" short for in Harry S Truman's name?

6. Who was the first President inaugurated in Washington, DC?

7. Who was the first President to survive an assassination attempt?

8. Who was the shortest President?

9. Who was the first President to lead the US army into battle?

10. Which President was the first American to win a Nobel Prize?

Answer Sheet   Answer Sheet   Answer Sheet

Presidents 2 Rolls	Presidents 2 Rolls	Presidents 2 Rolls
Name_____	Name_____	Name_____

1.	1.	1.
2.	2.	2.
3.	3.	3.
4.	4.	4.
5.	5.	5.
6.	6.	6.
7.	7.	7.
8.	8.	8.
9.	9.	9.
10.	10.	10.

After you have filled out the sheet, fold your column underneath along the dashed line so the next restroom user won't see your answers. ***The first player uses the far right column.***

Notes: *Notes:*   *Notes:*

Presidents

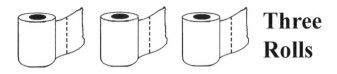

Three Rolls

Flip to pg. 82 for answers

1. Who promised a "full dinner pail?"

2. Who was the first President to have been divorced?

3. Who is sometimes given credit for inadvertently inventing the 7th inning stretch?

4. Which President got stuck in the White House bathtub and needed a team of men to help him out?

5. Who was the first President born in the US (earlier ones were born in the colonies)?

6. Who was the only *elected* President not chosen by the Electoral College or the House of Representatives?

7. Which President was taught to read and write by his wife?

8. Who was the only President from the Democratic Party between 1860 and 1912?

9. Who was the first President to be born in a hospital?

10. Who was the only President to later serve in the House of Representatives?

Answer Sheet

Presidents
3 Rolls

Name_____

Answer Sheet

Presidents
3 Rolls

Name_____

Answer Sheet

Presidents
3 Rolls

Name_____

1.	1.	1.
2.	2.	2.
3.	3.	3.
4.	4.	4.
5.	5.	5.
6.	6.	6.
7.	7.	7.
8.	8.	8.
9.	9.	9.
10.	10.	10.

After you have filled out the sheet, fold your column underneath along the dashed line so the next restroom user won't see your answers. *The first player uses the far right column.*

Notes: *Notes:*   *Notes:*

Vice-Presidents

 ## One Roll

Flip to pg. 83 for answers

1. This VP couldn't spell "potato."

2. She was the first woman to be chosen as a VP candidate by a major party.

3. Who was the first VP?

4. Who was Franklin Delano Roosevelt's last VP?

5. Who was Ronald Reagan's VP for both his terms?

6. If the President and VP both die, who is next in line for the Presidency?

7. When President McKinley died in 1901, who became President?

8. Which 20th Century VP would be erroneously considered "accident prone" after he became President?

9. After being VP, he won an Oscar for an environmental film.

10. When President Kennedy was assassinated in 1963, which VP became President?

Answer Sheet

Vice-Presidents
1 Roll

Name_____

Answer Sheet

Vice-Presidents
1 Roll

Name_____

Answer Sheet

Vice-Presidents
1 Roll

Name_____

1.	1.	1.
2.	2.	2.
3.	3.	3.
4.	4.	4.
5.	5.	5.
6.	6.	6.
7.	7.	7.
8.	8.	8.
9.	9.	9.
10.	10.	10.

After you have filled out the sheet, fold your column underneath along the dashed line so the next restroom user won't see your answers. *The first player uses the far right column.*

Notes:

Notes:

Notes:

Vice-Presidents

Two Rolls

Flip to pg. 84 for answers

1. Who committed a murder while VP?

2. Republican Abraham Lincoln picked a Democrat as his second VP. Who was he?

3. When President Harding died in 1923, who became President?

4. Which VP resigned after pleading no contest to income tax evasion?

5. When VP Ford became President, who was chosen to be the new VP?

6. The grandson of Grover Cleveland's VP ran for President in 1952 and 1956. Who was he?

7. Who was the first VP to later become President?

8. Who was Lyndon Johnson's VP from 1965-69?

9. Who was the first VP to be a member of a different political party than the President?

10. Madison's VP was known for re-drawing Congressional districts while he was governor of Massachusetts. Who was he?

Answer Sheet

Vice-Presidents
2 Rolls

Name_____

1.
2.
3.
4.
5.
6.
7.
8.
9.
10.

Answer Sheet

Vice-Presidents
2 Rolls

Name_____

1.
2.
3.
4.
5.
6.
7.
8.
9.
10.

Answer Sheet

Vice-Presidents
2 Rolls

Name_____

1.
2.
3.
4.
5.
6.
7.
8.
9.
10.

After you have filled out the sheet, fold your column underneath along the dashed line so the next restroom user won't see your answers. *The first player uses the far right column.*

Notes:

Notes:

Notes:

Vice-Presidents

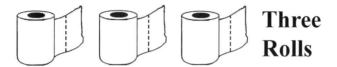

Three Rolls

Flip to pg. 85 for answers

1. Who was Abraham Lincoln's first VP?

2. Which VP was once a member of the House Un-American Activities Committee?

3. Who was the first VP to serve under two different presidents and the first to die in office?

4. Who was the first VP to become Chief Executive following the death of the President?

5. Which VP said that the Vice Presidency is a "spare tire on the automobile of government"?

6. Until 1967, if the office of VP was vacant, who became the VP?

7. Which VP was a key figure in the Crédit Mobilier scandal?

8. John Quincy Adams' and Jackson's VP was a southern states rights leader. Who was he?

9. When President Garfield was assassinated in 1881, which VP became President?

10. Which VP said, "What this country needs is a good five cent cigar"?

Answer Sheet   Answer Sheet   Answer Sheet

Vice-Presidents
3 Rolls

Vice-Presidents
3 Rolls

Vice-Presidents
3 Rolls

Name_____   Name_____   Name_____

1.	1.	1.
2.	2.	2.
3.	3.	3.
4.	4.	4.
5.	5.	5.
6.	6.	6.
7.	7.	7.
8.	8.	8.
9.	9.	9.
10.	10.	10.

After you have filled out the sheet, fold your column underneath along the dashed line so the next restroom user won't see your answers. ***The first player uses the far right column.***

Notes: *Notes:*   *Notes:*

Dates (Just the year, thank you)

 One Roll

Flip to pg. 86 for answers

1. D-Day

2. Declaration of Independence signed

3. Kennedy Assassination

4. Lee surrenders to Grant

5. Man walks on the moon

6. The Nixon-Kennedy Debates

7. Al Gore concedes the Presidency to George Bush

8. Stock Market Crash triggers the Great Depression

9. Battle of Gettysburg

10. Super Bowl I

Answer Sheet

Dates
1 Roll

Name_____

Answer Sheet

Dates
1 Roll

Name_____

Answer Sheet

Dates
1 Roll

Name_____

1.	1.	1.
2.	2.	2.
3.	3.	3.
4.	4.	4.
5.	5.	5.
6.	6.	6.
7.	7.	7.
8.	8.	8.
9.	9.	9.
10.	10.	10.

After you have filled out the sheet, fold your column underneath along the dashed line so the next restroom user won't see your answers. ***The first player uses the far right column.***

Notes: *Notes:*   *Notes:*

Dates (Just the year, thank you)

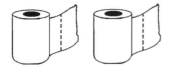 **Two Rolls**

Flip to pg. 87 for answers

1. V-E Day

2. Titanic sinks

3. Gettysburg Address

4. "I Have a Dream" Speech

5. Miracle on Ice

6. Armistice declared ending World War I

7. Bill Clinton impeached

8. Saddam Hussein is captured by American forces

9. Lincoln Assassination

10. George Washington is inaugurated as the first US President

Answer Sheet   Answer Sheet   Answer Sheet

Dates   **Dates**   **Dates**
2 Rolls   **2 Rolls**   **2 Rolls**

Name_____   Name_____   Name_____

1.	1.	1.
2.	2.	2.
3.	3.	3.
4.	4.	4.
5.	5.	5.
6.	6.	6.
7.	7.	7.
8.	8.	8.
9.	9.	9.
10.	10.	10.

After you have filled out the sheet, fold your column underneath along the dashed line so the next restroom user won't see your answers. ***The first player uses the far right column.***

Notes: *Notes:*   *Notes:*

Dates (Just the year, thank you)

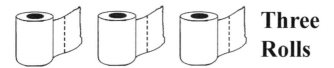 **Three Rolls**

Flip to pg. 88 for answers

Special rule for Dates-Three Rolls only. Get within 3 years either way.

1. Golden Spike is hammered at Promontory Summit, Utah

2. Triangle Shirtwaist Fire

3. Social Security is created

4. Jackie Robinson plays first game in the Major Leagues

5. Brooklyn Bridge opens

6. The Beatles perform for the first time at Shea Stadium

7. Beginning of the Korean War

8. Lindbergh crosses the Atlantic

9. Rosa Parks rides the bus, challenging segregation

10. Alexander Hamilton and Aaron Burr duel

Answer Sheet | Answer Sheet | Answer Sheet

| Dates
3 Rolls | Dates
3 Rolls | Dates
3 Rolls |

Name_____ Name_____ Name_____

1.	1.	1.
2.	2.	2.
3.	3.	3.
4.	4.	4.
5.	5.	5.
6.	6.	6.
7.	7.	7.
8.	8.	8.
9.	9.	9.
10.	10.	10.

After you have filled out the sheet, fold your column underneath along the dashed line so the next restroom user won't see your answers. *The first player uses the far right column.*

Notes: | *Notes:* | *Notes:*

Sports

One Roll

Flip to pg. 89 for answers

1. What early football star was known as "The Galloping Ghost?"

2. Who has won the most Grand Slam Tennis Championships in Men's Tennis history?

3. Who won Super Bowl I?

4. What team has won the most NBA championships?

5. Who held the record for most home runs in a career before Barry Bonds?

6. What is the name of the trophy given to the top college football player?

7. What incredibly famous auto race on Memorial Day Weekend usually has the victor drinking milk in the Winner's Circle?

8. What are the four events that constitute golf's Grand Slam?

9. Who is the only Major League Baseball team to relinquish a 3-0 lead in games during post-season play?

10. What three categories make up baseball's Triple Crown?

Answer Sheet

Sports
1 Roll

Name_____

Answer Sheet

Sports
1 Roll

Name_____

Answer Sheet

Sports
1 Roll

Name_____

1.	1.	1.
2.	2.	2.
3.	3.	3.
4.	4.	4.
5.	5.	5.
6.	6.	6.
7.	7.	7.
8.	8.	8.
9.	9.	9.
10.	10.	10.

After you have filled out the sheet, fold your column underneath along the dashed line so the next restroom user won't see your answers. ***The first player uses the far right column.***

Notes: *Notes:*   *Notes:*

Sports

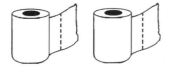 **Two Rolls**

Flip to pg. 90 for answers

1. Who was the coach of the 1980 "Miracle on Ice" US Olympic hockey team?

2. Who was the "Brown Bomber?"

3. Who hit the "Shot Heard 'Round the World"?

4. Who was Johnny Most?

5. Who was the last team to win four consecutive Stanley Cups?

6. Where did the A's play before they moved to Oakland?

7. Who coached the Dallas Cowboys to Super Bowl victories in 1972 and 1978?

8. Who overcame an injury and made a surprise start to lead the NY Knicks to the 1969-70 NBA title?

9. What was Kareem Abdul Jabbar's birth name?

10. Who hit the ball through Bill Buckner's legs in the 1986 World Series?

Answer Sheet

Sports
2 Rolls

Name_____

1.
2.
3.
4.
5.
6.
7.
8.
9.
10.

Answer Sheet

Sports
2 Rolls

Name_____

1.
2.
3.
4.
5.
6.
7.
8.
9.
10.

Answer Sheet

Sports
2 Rolls

Name_____

1.
2.
3.
4.
5.
6.
7.
8.
9.
10.

After you have filled out the sheet, fold your column underneath along the dashed line so the next restroom user won't see your answers. ***The first player uses the far right column.***

Notes: *Notes:*   *Notes:*

Sports

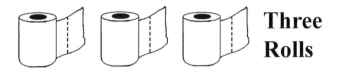

Three Rolls

Flip to pg. 91 for answers

1. Who did Lou Gehrig replace at the start of his 4,130 consecutive game streak?

2. Before Flushing Meadows, where was the US Tennis Open played?

3. What former President was once a broadcaster for the Chicago Cubs?

4. In what stadium did the Pittsburgh Pirates play from 1909-1970?

5. Who were the Steagles?

6. Who said, "Win this one for the Gipper"?

7. What football Hall-of-Famer and coach/owner played right field for the Yankees before Babe Ruth?

8. What was the original name of the basketball league that later became the NBA?

9. What were the first two baseball "expansion teams" in 1961?

10. Who was the first US-based team to win the Stanley Cup?

Answer Sheet

Sports
3 Rolls

Name_____

Answer Sheet

Sports
3 Rolls

Name_____

Answer Sheet

Sports
3 Rolls

Name_____

1.	1.	1.
2.	2.	2.
3.	3.	3.
4.	4.	4.
5.	5.	5.
6.	6.	6.
7.	7.	7.
8.	8.	8.
9.	9.	9.
10.	10.	10.

After you have filled out the sheet, fold your column underneath along the dashed line so the next restroom user won't see your answers. *The first player uses the far right column.*

Notes:

Notes:

Notes:

Wars

 **One Roll**

Flip to
pg. 92
for
answers

1. What was the bloodiest war (deaths) in American History?

2. In what war was the poem that became *The Star Spangled Banner* written?

3. Who was the leader of the Confederate army?

4. On what date was Pearl Harbor attacked?

5. Who was the Communist leader of North Vietnam?

6. Where was the first shot of the Civil War fired?

7. What were the *two* Japanese cities virtually destroyed by atomic bombs in 1945?

8. What does V-E day stand for?

9. In which war did Harry Truman fire General Douglas MacArthur?

10. What was the nickname that European soldiers used to refer to WWI US troops of the American Expeditionary Forces? One might say they were ticklish in their stomachs.

Answer Sheet

Wars
1 Roll

Name_____

	Answer Sheet — Wars 1 Roll — Name	Answer Sheet — Wars 1 Roll — Name
1.	1.	1.
2.	2.	2.
3.	3.	3.
4.	4.	4.
5.	5.	5.
6.	6.	6.
7.	7.	7.
8.	8.	8.
9.	9.	9.
10.	10.	10.

After you have filled out the sheet, fold your column underneath along the dashed line so the next restroom user won't see your answers. ***The first player uses the far right column.***

Notes: *Notes:*   *Notes:*

Wars

Two Rolls

Flip to pg. 93 for answers

1. Where was the famous WWII photo of US Marines triumphantly raising the American flag taken?

2. What Civil War General are prostitutes named for?

3. Which foreign war caused the first *peacetime* draft in American History?

4. What was the name of President George H.W. Bush's operation in Iraq?

5. Which war saw the Tet Offensive?

6. When were the "13 Days" of the Cuban Missile Crisis?

7. Where did General Cornwallis surrender the British Army in the Revolutionary War?

8. After what war did the "Executive Mansion" become more popularly known as "The White House?"

9. What parallel was, and still is today, the separation of North and South Korea?

10. Who led the final Confederate charge at Gettysburg?

Answer Sheet

Wars
2 Rolls

Name_____

1.
2.
3.
4.
5.
6.
7.
8.
9.
10.

Answer Sheet

Wars
2 Rolls

Name_____

1.
2.
3.
4.
5.
6.
7.
8.
9.
10.

Answer Sheet

Wars
2 Rolls

Name_____

1.
2.
3.
4.
5.
6.
7.
8.
9.
10.

After you have filled out the sheet, fold your column underneath along the dashed line so the next restroom user won't see your answers. *The first player uses the far right column.*

Notes:

Notes:

Notes:

Wars

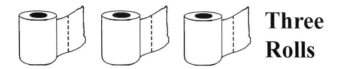 **Three Rolls**

Flip to pg. 94 for answers

1. When was the first time American troops fought outside of North America?

2. Who is given credit for leading the final Oglala Sioux attack on George Armstrong Custer's troops at Little Bighorn in 1876?

3. After entering Paris during WWI, what American said, "Lafayette, we are here"?

4. Which conflict saw the first *wartime* draft in American History?

5. Who surrendered to whom at the Battle of Saratoga?

6. What young British officer, who later became a world-wide household name, helped start the French and Indian War?

7. What war gave the US land that would one day become California?

8. Who was the hero of Little Round Top (Battle of Gettysburg)?

9. Why was the Battle of New Orleans really a military afterthought?

10. Which boat was sunk, thus triggering the Spanish-American War?

Answer Sheet | Answer Sheet | Answer Sheet

Wars	**Wars**	**Wars**
3 Rolls	**3 Rolls**	**3 Rolls**

Name_____ Name_____ Name_____

1.	1.	1.
2.	2.	2.
3.	3.	3.
4.	4.	4.
5.	5.	5.
6.	6.	6.
7.	7.	7.
8.	8.	8.
9.	9.	9.
10.	10.	10.

After you have filled out the sheet, fold your column underneath along the dashed line so the next restroom user won't see your answers. ***The first player uses the far right column.***

Notes: | *Notes:* | *Notes:*

Pop Culture

 **One Roll**

Flip to pg. 95 for answers

1. What was the first all day cable news network?

2. What famous jazz musician was nicknamed Satchmo?

3. The Buggles' *Video Killed the Radio Star* was the first song to be played on what new 1981 TV network?

4. Name one of the two games that were included in the Nintendo Entertainment System. One of the games needed the *Zapper*.

5. What is the longest running game show on television?

6. What is the longest running Broadway show of all time?

7. What 1939 classic movie had been rumored for decades to contain a suicide occurring in the background?

8. What is the highest grossing movie of all time?

9. Who was the anchor of the CBS Evening News for 19 years? Many called him the "Most Trusted Man in America."

10. On what classic television sitcom did Ralph Kramden violently threaten to send his wife to the moon?

Answer Sheet

Pop Culture
1 Roll

Name_____

Answer Sheet

Pop Culture
1 Roll

Name_____

Answer Sheet

Pop Culture
1 Roll

Name_____

1.	1.	1.
2.	2.	2.
3.	3.	3.
4.	4.	4.
5.	5.	5.
6.	6.	6.
7.	7.	7.
8.	8.	8.
9.	9.	9.
10.	10.	10.

After you have filled out the sheet, fold your column underneath along the dashed line so the next restroom user won't see your answers. *The first player uses the far right column.*

Notes:

Notes:

Notes:

Pop Culture

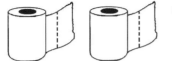

Two Rolls

Flip to pg. 96 for answers

1. What 1927 Al Jolson full featured film was the first "talkie" in American History?

2. What television show is *The Simpsons* a spin-off of?

3. How many dice are rolled at one time in Yahtzee?

4. What were Messrs. Yarrow and Stookey, and Ms. Travers better known as?

5. How many *Star Wars* movies were there?

6. Who is the Baby Ruth candy bar named for?

7. Who hosted *Jeopardy!* before Alex Trebeck?

8. What show was Abraham Lincoln attending when he was assassinated in 1865?

9. In what city was *American Bandstand* originally broadcast from?

10. What beer made Milwaukee famous?

Answer Sheet | Answer Sheet | Answer Sheet

Pop Culture
2 Rolls

Pop Culture
2 Rolls

Pop Culture
2 Rolls

Name_____ Name_____ Name_____

1.	1.	1.
2.	2.	2.
3.	3.	3.
4.	4.	4.
5.	5.	5.
6.	6.	6.
7.	7.	7.
8.	8.	8.
9.	9.	9.
10.	10.	10.

After you have filled out the sheet, fold your column underneath along the dashed line so the next restroom user won't see your answers. ***The first player uses the far right column.***

Notes: *Notes:*   *Notes:*

Pop Culture

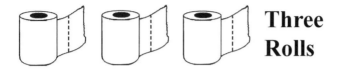

Three Rolls

Flip to pg. 97 for answers

1. What 1915 D.W. Griffith movie portrayed the KKK as heroes, and was shown by Woodrow Wilson in the White House?

2. What was the first commercial radio station in the United States?

3. What was used as a special effect for blood in the shower scene in Alfred Hitchcock's *Psycho*?

4. *The Wizard of Oz* was a political statement. What did Oz stand for?

5. One of this person's favorite sandwiches was "Fool's Gold Loaf," a sandwich consisting of hollowed out bread, jam, peanut butter, and bacon. Who was he?

6. *The Anacreontic Song* was added to a poem to create what famous ballad?

7. Who lived at 1313 Mockingbird Lane?

8. Who were the three comedians that hosted the first HBO *Comic Relief*?

9. Moses Horowitz, Jerome Horowitz, and Louis Feinberg, are better known as whom?

10. In what town on Earth did *Superman* grow up?

Answer Sheet

Pop Culture
3 Rolls

Name_____

Answer Sheet

Pop Culture
3 Rolls

Name_____

Answer Sheet

Pop Culture
3 Rolls

Name_____

1.	1.	1.
2.	2.	2.
3.	3.	3.
4.	4.	4.
5.	5.	5.
6.	6.	6.
7.	7.	7.
8.	8.	8.
9.	9.	9.
10.	10.	10.

After you have filled out the sheet, fold your column underneath along the dashed line so the next restroom user won't see your answers. *The first player uses the far right column.*

Notes:

Notes:

Notes:

The Road to Independence

 ## One Roll — Answers

1. Thomas Paine wrote this in his pamphlet, *The American Crisis,* Dec. 23, 1776. He was writing to raise the morale of the American troops.

2. Samuel Adams

3. Hessians

4. Lexington, MA

5. Patrick Henry

6. Two. One if by land. Two if by sea.

7. Philadelphia, PA

8. George III

9. Benedict Arnold

10. Native Americans

The Road to Independence

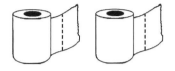 **Two Rolls — Answers**

1. Alexander Hamilton

2. Samuel Adams and John Hancock

3. John Adams, Benjamin Franklin, Roger Sherman, Robert Livingston

4. Gilbert du Motier, Marquis de Lafayette (or just plain Lafayette will do)

5. The Battle of Long Island (originally called the Battle of Brooklyn)

6. The Articles of Confederation

7. Tories

8. Boston and New York

9. So the King could read it without his glasses. Note that there is absolutely no evidence that these words were ever uttered.

10. A turkey

The Road to Independence

Three Rolls —
Answers

1. 56

2. 342 cases of tea

3. Nathan Hale

4. General Thomas Gage

5. Fort Ticonderoga on Lake Champlain

6. Andrew Jackson

7. Crispus Attucks, a free black

8. John Adams

9. The Conway Cabal

10. Casimir Pulaski

The Young Nation

 ## One Roll — Answers

1. None. Of course only the few members of the Electoral College voted in those days.

2. Henry Knox

3. The War of 1812

4. John Adams

5. James Madison

6. John Jay

7. Sacagawea. She did not speak English, but rather could translate Shoshone to Hidatsa, and then communicate with her husband, who spoke Hidatsa and French.

8. *Old Ironsides*. The ship was actually made of wood. Very hard wood.

9. Andrew Jackson

10. Vermont

The Young Nation

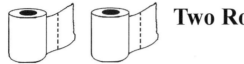

Two Rolls — Answers

1. On the steps of old City Hall in New York City

2. John Adams and Thomas Jefferson. According to eyewitnesses, Adams' last words were, "Thomas Jefferson survives." He was wrong, as Jefferson passed away a few hours earlier.

3. Overlooking Ft. McHenry in Baltimore, MD

4. Shays' Rebellion

5. New York City, Philadelphia, Washington, DC

6. The Federalists and the Anti-Federalists (also known as the Democratic-Republicans, National Republicans, and Republicans)

7. 3/5

8. 1800. After many ballots, the House of Representatives chose Thomas Jefferson over Aaron Burr. Because of the original wording of the Constitution, Burr became Vice-President. Electors began choosing a President and a Vice-President together after the passage of the 12th Amendment in 1804.

9. Aaron Burr. After the duel with Alexander Hamilton, Burr fled west, and hatched an alleged failed plot to get the western states and New England to secede. With John Marshall presiding at his treason trial, Burr was acquitted in 1807.

10. Dolley Madison

The Young Nation

Three Rolls — Answers

1. Thomas Jefferson and James Madison. Jefferson was Vice-President at the time.

2. $15 million

3. Weehawken, NJ—not far from where the first modern game of baseball was played in neighboring Hoboken on June 19, 1846. Burr and Hamilton had to paddle over to NJ because dueling was illegal in NY. Hamilton helped pass that law after his oldest son, Phillip, had died in a duel a few years earlier.

4. Pennsylvania

5. 55 representatives from 12 states. Rhode Island wasn't interested.

6. Alexander Hamilton and James Madison met with Thomas Jefferson at the latter's home to work out a deal whereby the permanent capital of the US would be on the Potomac River, and the Federal Government would assume the Revolutionary War debts of the states.

7. Charles-Maurice de Talleyrand-Périgord, 1st Prince de Benevent (or Talleyrand, for short)

8. John Dickinson

9. John Hanson

10. Edmond "Citizen" Genêt

The Civil War

 ## One Roll — Answers

1. Sept. 17, 1862. Battle of Antietam at Sharpsburg, MD. There were 22,720 casualties, including about 3,650 killed.

2. Battle of Gettysburg, July 1-3, 1863

3. The *Monitor* (Union) and the *Merrimack* (Confederacy). Actually, the Confederate ship was called the *Virginia* by that time, but most people still refer to that battle as the *Monitor* vs. the *Merrimack*.

4. 1861-1865

5. Jefferson Davis

6. South Carolina

7. Greenbacks

8. Massachusetts

9. Stonewall

10. Appomattox Courthouse, VA

The Civil War

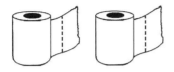 ## Two Rolls — Answers

1. Abner Doubleday. Baseball historians today agree that he did *not* invent baseball in 1839 at Cooperstown, NY as many originally believed.

2. 13

3. Grant the Butcher

4. Richmond

5. Shoes

6. George McClellan

7. *Sic semper tyrannis* (Thus always to tyrants)

8. *Dixie.* Daniel Decatur Emmett was born in Ohio. He later said that if he knew the South was going to adopt the song, he never would have written it!

9. New York City

10. Anaconda

The Civil War

1. None. In writing, the Emancipation Proclamation only freed slaves in the rebelling states...you know, those states that stopped listening to the Federal Government after seceding.

2. Winfield Scott, the aged hero of the Mexican War

3. Quantrill's Raiders

4. Wilmer McLean. After the Battle of Bull Run tore up his farm in 1861, he fled for safety to Appomattox Courthouse, VA. Yet, the war followed him. For this was where Lee surrendered to Grant in 1865... at McLean's new house! It has been said that the Civil War started in his yard, and ended in his parlor.

5. The roads were clogged with picnickers. Many Washingtonians felt that the battle would be "entertainment," and traveled out to watch the war. Needless to say, they left in a panic.

6. Battle of the Crater, July 30, 1864 during the Siege of Petersburg, VA. The Union detonated a mine, creating a huge explosion. However, the Union soldiers were too confused to fight efficiently, and the Confederacy quickly recovered. More Union soldiers died in the battle than Confederates.

7. The Laird Rams. The Union and Britain almost went to war over this issue.

8. Benjamin Butler

9. Chattanooga, TN and Chickamauga, GA

10. Antietam (or Sharpsburg)

The 20th Century

 ## One Roll — Answers

1. Lance Ito

2. The *Hindenburg*

3. The St. Valentine's Day Massacre

4. *Brown v. Board of Education*

5. The *Lusitania*

6. Roswell, NM

7. Thanksgiving

8. Flappers

9. Ronald Reagan

10. John F. Kennedy. He thought he was saying in German, "I am a Berliner," but didn't realize that "Berliner" meant jelly doughnut.

The 20th Century

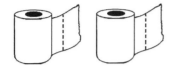 **Two Rolls — Answers**

1. The *Spirit of St. Louis*

2. The *Enola Gay*

3. The Progressive Party (also called the Bull Moose Party)

4. *The Jungle*

5. Mark David Chapman

6. The Chrysler Building at 1,046 feet. The Empire State Building opened a year later.

7. Fala

8. From left to right, George Washington, Thomas Jefferson, Theodore Roosevelt, Abraham Lincoln

9. "Star Wars"

10. Mt. St. Helens

The 20th Century

Three Rolls — Answers

1. Clarence Darrow for the defense, William Jennings Bryan for the prosecution

2. The Dust Bowl

3. Theodore Roosevelt in 1906, when he visited the construction site of the Panama Canal

4. Symbolics.com, registered March 15, 1985

5. Wham-O

6. Ludlow, CO

7. Francis Gary Powers

8. Secretary of the Interior, Albert Fall. This is where the expression, "Fall Guy" started.

9. George Marshall (The Marshall Plan)

10. He was shot on his way to deliver a speech in Milwaukee. He refused to go to the hospital until he finished giving his speech, which went on for about an hour. But it was perhaps the length of the speech that saved his life. The bullet's impact was slowed down considerably by the eyeglass case and folded speech in his shirt pocket. He said after speaking, "It takes more than that to kill a Bull Moose."

Presidents

 ## One Roll — Answers

1. William Henry Harrison, one month (March 4, 1841-April 4, 1841)

2. George Washington, as eulogized by Henry Lee

3. John F. Kennedy

4. Andrew Johnson

5. Abraham Lincoln

6. Grover Cleveland, 1885-1889 and 1893-1897

7. John Adams

8. Thomas Jefferson

9. Dwight D. Eisenhower

10. Franklin Delano Roosevelt

Presidents

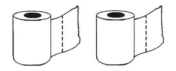

Two Rolls — Answers

1. James K. Polk

2. Andrew Jackson

3. James Monroe

4. Calvin Coolidge

5. Nothing. Just plain S. It seems that his mother's relatives were battling his father's relatives over what his middle name should be. Since both family names began with S, they compromised and essentially made his middle name S.

6. Thomas Jefferson

7. Andrew Jackson. On Jan. 30, 1835, Richard Lawrence pulled out two pistols and fired at the President. Both misfired. Later tests revealed that they should have worked.

8. James Madison – 5 ft. 4 in.

9. George Washington, at the start of the Federal Government's retaliation for the Whiskey Rebellion in 1794

10. Theodore Roosevelt won for his efforts to bring peace following the 1904-05 Russo-Japanese War

Presidents

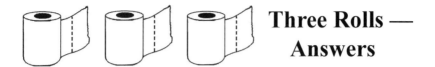

Three Rolls — Answers

1. William McKinley

2. Ronald Reagan

3. William H. Taft. According to legend, he stood up to stretch his large body in the 7th inning at a Washington Senators game, and everyone got up out of respect.

4. William H. Taft again. He really got a-round.

5. Martin Van Buren

6. Rutherford B. Hayes. Hayes, the Republican, was chosen by a special electoral commission following the disputed Election of 1876. The Electoral College could not decide between him and Samuel J. Tilden, the Democrat. Following a Constitutional debate, Congress decided to create the special commission to determine the winner. If you said Gerald Ford, sorry, he was never elected.

7. Andrew Johnson

8. Grover Cleveland

9. Jimmy Carter

10. John Quincy Adams

Vice-Presidents

 ## One Roll — Answers

1. Dan Quayle. Potatoe has no *e* at the end.

2. Geraldine Ferraro. She ran with Walter Mondale against Ronald Reagan in 1984.

3. John Adams

4. Harry S Truman

5. George H.W. Bush

6. The Speaker of the House of Representatives

7. Theodore Roosevelt. Republican leader Mark Hanna said, "Now look! That damned cowboy is President of the United States."

8. Gerald Ford was an All-American football player. But after he fell down the slippery steps of Air Force One, people seemed to forget that.

9. Al Gore won for *An Inconvenient Truth*

10. Lyndon Johnson

Vice-Presidents

 **Two Rolls — Answers**

1. No…not Dick Cheney. It was Aaron Burr. He shot Alexander Hamilton in a duel, and the former Treasury Secretary died a few days later.

2. Andrew Johnson. Although at the time Johnson was officially a member of the short-lived National Union Party.

3. Calvin Coolidge

4. Spiro Agnew in 1973

5. Nelson Rockefeller

6. Adlai Stevenson

7. John Adams

8. Hubert Humphrey

9. Thomas Jefferson. President John Adams was a Federalist. Jefferson was a Democratic-Republican.

10. Elbridge Gerry. (That's Gerry with a hard "g.") Even today, the re-drawing of Congressional districts to aid the party in power is known as gerrymandering (soft "g").

Vice-Presidents

 **Three Rolls —
Answers**

1. Hannibal Hamlin

2. Richard Nixon

3. George Clinton served under Thomas Jefferson and James Madison, and died in 1812

4. John Tyler, upon the death of President William Henry Harrison on April 4, 1841

5. John Nance Garner, who served under FDR for his first two terms. That's what he said when there were ladies present. To an all-male crowd, he generally said the "Vice Presidency ain't worth a bucket of warm piss."

6. Nobody. The 25th amendment, ratified in 1967, allows the President to appoint a VP with the confirmation of both houses of Congress.

7. Schuyler Colfax, Grant's VP for his first term

8. John C. Calhoun

9. Chester A. Arthur

10. Thomas Marshall, Woodrow Wilson's VP

Dates (Just the year, thank you)

 ## One Roll — Answers

1. 1944

2. 1776

3. 1963

4. 1865

5. 1969

6. 1960

7. 2000

8. 1929

9. 1863

10. 1967

Dates (Just the year, thank you)

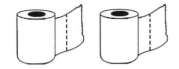 **Two Rolls — Answers**

1. 1945

2. 1912

3. 1863

4. 1963

5. 1980

6. 1918. 11th month, 11th day, 11th hour.

7. 1998

8. 2003

9. 1865

10. 1789

Dates (Just the year, thank you)

Three Rolls — Answers

1. 1869. The honor went to Leland Stanford of the Central Pacific Railroad. He swung and missed.

2. 1911

3. 1935

4. 1947

5. 1883

6. 1965. They also performed there in 1966.

7. 1950

8. 1927

9. 1955

10. 1804

Sports

 ## One Roll — Answers

1. Red Grange

2. Roger Federer—16. 5 US Open Titles, 6 Wimbledon Titles, 1 French Open Title, 4 Australian Open Titles.

3. The Green Bay Packers defeated the Kansas City Chiefs 35-10 in the first AFL-NFL Championship Game. It wasn't called the Super Bowl until later.

4. Boston Celtics – 17

5. Hank Aaron – 755

6. The Heisman Trophy

7. The Indianapolis 500

8. The Masters, US Open, British Open, PGA Championship

9. NY Yankees. They lost to the Boston Red Sox in the ALCS in 2004 after leading 3 games to 0. The Sox finally exorcised the "Curse of the Bambino."

10. Batting average, home runs, runs batted in

Sports

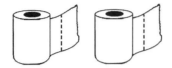 **Two Rolls — Answers**

1. Herb Brooks

2. Joe Louis

3. Bobby Thomson

4. Gravel-voiced announcer for the Boston Celtics

5. New York Islanders, 1980-1983

6. Kansas City. And before that, Philadelphia.

7. Tom Landry

8. Willis Reed

9. Lew Alcindor

10. Mookie Wilson

Sports

Three Rolls — Answers

1. Wally Pipp

2. Forest Hills

3. Ronald Reagan

4. Forbes Field

5. A combined team of Philadelphia Eagles and Pittsburgh Steelers in war-ravaged 1943

6. Knute Rockne

7. George Halas, much more famous as the owner and coach of the Chicago Bears. He played a few games for the Yankees in 1919. However it would be presumptive to claim that he was *the* regular right fielder before the Babe.

8. Basketball Association of America (BAA). Critics called it the "sheep league" for obvious reasons.

9. Los Angeles Angels and the "second" Washington Senators, who replaced the old DC team which had moved to Minnesota

10. Seattle Metropolitans, 1917

Wars

 One Roll — Answers

1. The Civil War, with over 600,000 Americans killed

2. The War of 1812

3. Robert E. Lee

4. December 7, 1941

5. Ho Chi Minh

6. Ft. Sumter in Charleston, SC harbor

7. "Little Boy" was dropped by the *Enola Gay* on Hiroshima on Aug. 6th, and "Fat Man" was dropped by *Bockscar* on Nagasaki on Aug. 9th

8. Victory in Europe

9. The Korean War

10. Doughboys

Wars

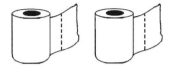 ## Two Rolls — Answers

1. At Mt. Suribachi on the island of Iwo Jima

2. Union General Joseph Hooker. Actually, prostitutes were sometimes called hookers in those days, but the general's penchant for the ladies of the evening popularized it.

3. World War II

4. Desert Storm

5. The Vietnam War

6. October, 1962

7. Yorktown, VA

8. The War of 1812. After the British set fire to it, the Executive Mansion got a fresh coat of white paint.

9. 38°

10. General George Pickett. The final, unsuccessful assault became known as "Pickett's Charge."

Wars

Three Rolls — Answers

1. Tripoli. American troops under Stephen Decatur defeated the Barbary Pirates along the northern coast of Africa in 1804.

2. Crazy Horse

3. Gen. John Pershing was first given credit for this quote, but he later admitted that it was said by Col. Charles E. Stanton at the tomb of Lafayette on July 4, 1917. Col. Stanton was the nephew of Lincoln's Secretary of War, Edwin M. Stanton. But good news! We'll accept Pershing as the correct answer.

4. The Civil War

5. British General John Burgoyne surrendered to American General Horatio Gates on Oct. 17, 1777

6. George Washington. He was involved in skirmishes near modern day Pittsburgh in 1754. Remember...American colonists were British back then!

7. The Mexican War

8. Joshua Lawrence Chamberlain of Maine. Honorable Mention to Gouverneur Kemble Warren of New York.

9. The battle was fought after a peace treaty was signed in Ghent, Belgium. But in the absence of CNN, no one knew.

10. USS *Maine*. Most Americans assumed that Spain had planted a bomb on the ship and demanded war. However modern technology has proven that the explosion was internal and likely an accident.

Pop Culture

 ## One Roll — Answers

1. CNN

2. Louis Armstrong

3. MTV

4. *Super Mario Bros.* and *Duck Hunt*

5. *The Price is Right*. The current version began in 1972. An earlier show ran from 1956-1965, hosted by Bill Cullen.

6. *The Phantom of the Opera*. It passed *Cats* in 2006. Cats closed with 7,485 performances in 2000 after an 18-year run. As of mid-2011, *The Phantom of the Opera* was still playing on Broadway with over 10,000 performances dating back to 1988.

7. *The Wizard of Oz*. This rumor was debunked recently, as examining the film reveals an exotic bird spreading its wings, not a Munchkin hanging himself. The Munchkins were not even on the set yet, as the movie was filmed out of chronological order.

8. *Avatar.* It grossed 2.7 billion dollars in 2009.

9. Walter Cronkite

10. *The Honeymooners*. Threatening to hit your wife in the kisser probably wouldn't slide in Hollywood today.

Pop Culture

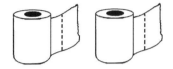 ## Two Rolls — Answers

1. *The Jazz Singer*

2. *The Tracey Ullman Show*

3. Five

4. Peter, Paul, and Mary

5. Six

6. Ruth Cleveland, President Grover Cleveland's daughter. Although the candy bar came out around the peak of Babe Ruth's career, he did not receive handsome royalties.

7. Art Fleming

8. *Our American Cousin*

9. Philadelphia

10. Schlitz

Pop Culture

Three Rolls — Answers

1. *The Birth of a Nation*

2. KDKA in Pittsburgh. Its first broadcast was coverage of Election Night 1920, in which Warren G. Harding defeated James Cox. The announcer asked that anyone listening should send a letter confirming they heard it.

3. Chocolate syrup. The movie was in black and white.

4. Ounces. The Wizard of Oz was an allegory of Populism and the Election of 1896 between Republican William McKinley and Democrat William Jennings Bryan. McKinley stood for gold. Bryan stood for silver. Both are measured in ounces. The Cowardly Lion was Bryan, the heartless Tin Man stood for the industrialists, and the Scarecrow represented the farmers. The Yellow Brick Road, of course, was gold.

5. Elvis Presley

6. *The Star Spangled Banner.* The hymn was added to Francis Scott Key's poem, *Defence of Fort McHenry,* to create the National Anthem.

7. *The Munsters*

8. Billy Crystal, Whoopi Goldberg, and Robin Williams

9. The Three Stooges

10. Smallville

Scorecard — Name: _____

Category	# Right		# of Pts.		Tot. Pts.
Road to Independence - 1 Roll		x	1	=	
Road to Independence - 2 Rolls		x	2	=	
Road to Independence - 3 Rolls		x	3	=	
Young Nation - 1 Roll		x	1	=	
Young Nation - 2 Rolls		x	2	=	
Young Nation - 3 Rolls		x	3	=	
Civil War - 1 Roll		x	1	=	
Civil War - 2 Rolls		x	2	=	
Civil War - 3 Rolls		x	3	=	
20th Century - 1 Roll		x	1	=	
20th Century - 2 Rolls		x	2	=	
20th Century - 3 Rolls		x	3	=	
Presidents - 1 Roll		x	1	=	
Presidents - 2 Rolls		x	2	=	
Presidents - 3 Rolls		x	3	=	
Vice-Presidents - 1 Roll		x	1	=	
Vice-Presidents - 2 Rolls		x	2	=	
Vice-Presidents - 3 Rolls		x	3	=	
Dates - 1 Roll		x	1	=	
Dates - 2 Rolls		x	2	=	
Dates - 3 Rolls		x	3	=	
Sports - 1 Roll		x	1	=	
Sports - 2 Rolls		x	2	=	
Sports - 3 Rolls		x	3	=	
Wars - 1 Roll		x	1	=	
Wars - 2 Rolls		x	2	=	
Wars - 3 Rolls		x	3	=	
Pop Culture - 1 Roll		x	1	=	
Pop Culture - 2 Rolls		x	2	=	
Pop Culture - 3 Rolls		x	3	=	

Grand Total

Scorecard — Name: _____

Category	# Right		# of Pts.		Tot. Pts.
Road to Independence - 1 Roll		x	1	=	
Road to Independence - 2 Rolls		x	2	=	
Road to Independence - 3 Rolls		x	3	=	
Young Nation - 1 Roll		x	1	=	
Young Nation - 2 Rolls		x	2	=	
Young Nation - 3 Rolls		x	3	=	
Civil War - 1 Roll		x	1	=	
Civil War - 2 Rolls		x	2	=	
Civil War - 3 Rolls		x	3	=	
20th Century - 1 Roll		x	1	=	
20th Century - 2 Rolls		x	2	=	
20th Century - 3 Rolls		x	3	=	
Presidents - 1 Roll		x	1	=	
Presidents - 2 Rolls		x	2	=	
Presidents - 3 Rolls		x	3	=	
Vice-Presidents - 1 Roll		x	1	=	
Vice-Presidents - 2 Rolls		x	2	=	
Vice-Presidents - 3 Rolls		x	3	=	
Dates - 1 Roll		x	1	=	
Dates - 2 Rolls		x	2	=	
Dates - 3 Rolls		x	3	=	
Sports - 1 Roll		x	1	=	
Sports - 2 Rolls		x	2	=	
Sports - 3 Rolls		x	3	=	
Wars - 1 Roll		x	1	=	
Wars - 2 Rolls		x	2	=	
Wars - 3 Rolls		x	3	=	
Pop Culture - 1 Roll		x	1	=	
Pop Culture - 2 Rolls		x	2	=	
Pop Culture - 3 Rolls		x	3	=	

Grand Total

Scorecard — Name: _____

Category	# Right		# of Pts.		Tot. Pts.
Road to Independence - 1 Roll		x	1	=	
Road to Independence - 2 Rolls		x	2	=	
Road to Independence - 3 Rolls		x	3	=	
Young Nation - 1 Roll		x	1	=	
Young Nation - 2 Rolls		x	2	=	
Young Nation - 3 Rolls		x	3	=	
Civil War - 1 Roll		x	1	=	
Civil War - 2 Rolls		x	2	=	
Civil War - 3 Rolls		x	3	=	
20th Century - 1 Roll		x	1	=	
20th Century - 2 Rolls		x	2	=	
20th Century - 3 Rolls		x	3	=	
Presidents - 1 Roll		x	1	=	
Presidents - 2 Rolls		x	2	=	
Presidents - 3 Rolls		x	3	=	
Vice-Presidents - 1 Roll		x	1	=	
Vice-Presidents - 2 Rolls		x	2	=	
Vice-Presidents - 3 Rolls		x	3	=	
Dates - 1 Roll		x	1	=	
Dates - 2 Rolls		x	2	=	
Dates - 3 Rolls		x	3	=	
Sports - 1 Roll		x	1	=	
Sports - 2 Rolls		x	2	=	
Sports - 3 Rolls		x	3	=	
Wars - 1 Roll		x	1	=	
Wars - 2 Rolls		x	2	=	
Wars - 3 Rolls		x	3	=	
Pop Culture - 1 Roll		x	1	=	
Pop Culture - 2 Rolls		x	2	=	
Pop Culture - 3 Rolls		x	3	=	

Grand Total

How did you do?

500 + — King/Queen of the Throne

400-499 — Topper of the Hopper

350-399 — Porcelain Prince/Princess

300-349 — Toileterrific!

250-299 — Keep Flushing for the Stars

200-249 — Might Need a Plunger

150-199 — Gotta call the Plumber

Below 150 — Clogged
Try a different Toiletrivia Book!

Made in the USA
San Bernardino, CA
23 December 2012